MONSTERS

BIGFOOT

BY HEATHER L. MILLER

KIDHAVEN PRESS

An imprint of Thomson Gale, a part of The Thomson Corporation

THOMSON

GALE

Detroit ¥ New York ¥ San Francisco ¥ San Diego
New Haven, Conn. ¥ Waterville, Maine ¥ London ¥ Munich

' 2006 Thomson Gale, a part of The Thomson Corporation.

Thomson and Star Logo are trademarks and Gale and KidHaven Press are registered trademarks used herein under license.

For more information, contact
KidHaven Press
27500 Drake Rd.
Farmington Hills, MI 48331-3535
Or you can visit our Internet site at http://www.gale.com

LIBRARY OF CONGRESS CATALOGING-IN-PUBLICATION DATA

Miller, Heather.
 Bigfoot / by Heather L. Miller.
   p. cm.   (Monsters)
 Includes bibliographical references and index.
 ISBN 0-7377-3161-3 (hardcover : alk. paper)
 1. Sasquatch Juvenile literature. I. Title. II. Monsters series (KidHaven Press).
QL89.2.S2M58 2005
001.944 dc22
 	
                   2004029423

Printed in the United States of America

CONTENTS

CHAPTER 1
Wanderer in the Woods   4

CHAPTER 2
Believable Beast?   13

CHAPTER 3
To Prove or Disprove   22

CHAPTER 4
Mystery and Merchandise   31

Notes   40

Glossary   42

For Further Exploration   43

Index   45

Picture Credits   47

About the Author   48

CHAPTER 1

WANDERER IN THE WOODS

On an October afternoon nearly forty years ago, the autumn breeze carried a strange scent through the majestic pine trees of northern California's Six Rivers National Forest. Two horses reared up in fear as the scent passed under their noses. One rider, Roger Patterson, was thrown to the ground. As Patterson raised his head from the dirt, his eyes met those of a large, hairy creature trudging through a clearing in the forest. Quickly, Patterson grabbed his home movie camera and followed what he believed was Bigfoot as it ran into the trees. Patterson was able to record several seconds of color footage of Bigfoot before it disappeared into the forest.

4

Patterson and his companion, Robert Gimlin, clutched the camera holding the precious evidence and followed the trail of Bigfoot's footprints back to their horses and out of the woods.

The evidence brought out of the forest on October 20, 1967, sparked heated debates about the possible existence of a large, hairy, apelike creature in

Bigfoot is an extremely large, apelike creature that people from all over the world have reported seeing.

the American Northwest. Today, people are still unsure if the evidence gathered that day was real. Nevertheless, the Patterson/Gimlin film brought Bigfoot into the American spotlight and forced many people to wonder if Bigfoot really exists.

Big Feet

The name Bigfoot is truly an appropriate name for the mysterious creature that supposedly left the 14½ x 6 inch (36.83 x 15.24 cm) footprints that Patterson and Gimlin found. But Bigfoot was actually tagged with this name nearly ten years before the Patterson/Gimlin sighting. On October 5, 1958, a bulldozer operator named Jerry Crew brought a plaster **cast** into a local newspaper office. He had made the cast of a footprint found near his worksite in Humboldt County, California. The *Humboldt Times* printed the headline "Bigfoot" along with a photograph of Crew and the footprint. Ever since that day the name Bigfoot has been used to describe a huge, hairy, upright-standing beast reportedly sighted in the United States.

Although the Pacific Northwest is most widely known for Bigfoot sightings, Bigfoot encounters have been reported all over the country. Sightings in the United States stretch from Alaska to New Mexico and Texas. Even midwestern states such as Indiana and Ohio have had reports of Bigfoot sightings.

Similar sightings have also been documented worldwide. Canadians have recorded sightings of a creature they call **Sasquatch** roaming through the

forests of British Columbia. Some people insist they have seen huge, hairy creatures roaming through the western mountains of Central and South America. Sightings of similar creatures known as **yeti** have been reported in China, Tibet, and Scotland.

LEGENDS OF LONG AGO

Just as records of Bigfoot, Sasquatch, or yeti sightings span the globe, legends of such a creature are strung throughout history. The epic poem *Beowulf,* written over a thousand years ago, tells of a great, terrifying creature called Grendel. Grendel captured people while they slept, took them away, and devoured them. Historians warn against interpreting this story

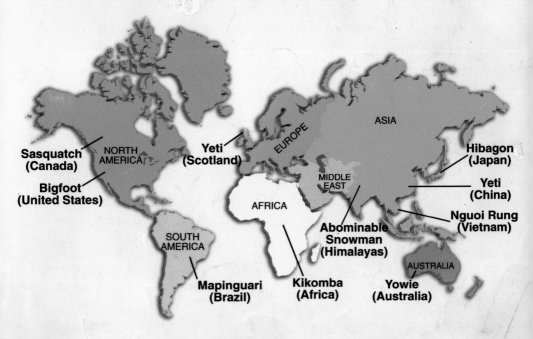

Bigfoot Names Around the World

Sasquatch (Canada)

NORTH AMERICA

Bigfoot (United States)

SOUTH AMERICA

Yeti (Scotland)

EUROPE

AFRICA

ASIA

MIDDLE EAST

Abominable Snowman (Himalayas)

Mapinguari (Brazil)

Kikomba (Africa)

Hibagon (Japan)

Yeti (China)

Nguoi Rung (Vietnam)

AUSTRALIA

Yowie (Australia)

Some Bigfoot enthusiasts believe that Grendel, the terrifying monster in the epic poem Beowulf, *was real.*

as true, but they also point out that many of the places and events described in the story are real. Bigfoot enthusiasts believe that although the stories in *Beowulf* may be exaggerated, the character Grendel could be based on an actual creature that did indeed terrorize the citizens of ancient Denmark.

Ancient Native American legends also mention Bigfoot creatures. The Yakama describe Bigfoot as an outcast who was transformed into an evil spirit named Qah-lin-me, which means "the devourer." The Hupa gave Bigfoot the name Omah, demon of the wilderness, to describe their feelings about the horrifying beast. A Native American story from 1871 tells of a young girl who was taken by Bigfoot while searching for firewood in the forest surrounding her village. She was held captive inside a hidden cave and was forced to live alongside the beast for over a year. The story goes on to say that after becoming ill, the girl returned to her village, where she gave birth to Bigfoot's baby.

TALL, DARK, AND HAIRY

Many Bigfoot enthusiasts believe that the widespread sightings, and stories of Bigfoot may actually describe encounters with eight or more different types of hairy **hominids** living throughout the world. The hominid theory assumes that early forms of humans still exist on Earth today and that Bigfoot sightings are actually accounts of modern humans meeting examples of primitive humans. Other Bigfoot enthusiasts believe that Bigfoot is simply an unknown species of gorilla, monkey, or ape.

The descriptions of Bigfoot could support either theory. People who claim to have seen Bigfoot tell of a large, hairy, **bipedal** creature with black to deep brown skin. Bigfoot's hair is usually described as long, especially the hair that hangs from the forearms, and it ranges in color from black to brown to reddish or even gray and white. Most Bigfoot reports tell of a tall creature that stands from 6 to 12 feet (2 to 4m) high with a large, barrel-like torso topped by a relatively small, pointed head. In a few accounts, the Bigfoot's teeth have been described as long and pointed. Its nose appears flattened and its eyes are small, round, and dark. In contrast to its small head, Bigfoot is almost always said to have extremely long arms and massive hands that have been compared to paddles.

Bigfoot's immense size is not its only outstanding feature. Many people who claim to have seen Bigfoot also report smelling an extremely foul odor. The smell has been compared to that of a skunk or burning rubber tires. One theory states that if Bigfoot does indeed throw off a foul smell, it does so as a means of communication.

Some enthusiasts believe that Bigfoot is capable of communicating with sounds. Moans, howls, hoots, grunts, and roars have been heard echoing through the forests and mountains where Bigfoot sightings have been reported. Enthusiasts can only guess what sort of messages Bigfoot may be sending, but some say it may be telling other Bigfoot creatures where to find food.

SUPER-SIZE MENU

Enthusiasts believe Bigfoot feasts on a wide variety of foods. Leaves, berries, fruit, and roots are some of the plants Bigfoot may eat. Fish, clams, crayfish,

People who claim to have seen Bigfoot say it is a hairy, bipedal creature with extremely long arms.

squirrel, elk, and bear are thought to be some of Bigfoot's favorite meat sources. Bigfoot does not appear to be a picky eater as it seems to choose rather unusual foods such as road kill or even garbage. In stories, the most unsettling item on Bigfoot's menu is human flesh.

Stories of Bigfoot behaviors and habits have been told for thousands of years. To those who claim to

Although Bigfoot is described as an enormous creature, its head is usually reported as small and pointed.

have seen the animal, there is no question of Bigfoot's existence. Others claim that the Bigfoot tales are merely stories that have been passed on by those who wish to keep the legend alive. Whichever the case, the idea of Bigfoot lives in the minds of those who choose to believe.

Bigfoot

CHAPTER 2

BELIEVABLE BEAST?

The stories of Bigfoot may sound like they were pulled straight off of movie screens or out of the fantasy section in the library. Many men and women have come out of North American forests and swamps telling their own hair-raising tales. Accounts of giant apes and wild, hairy men appear in American history from the early explorers to this very day. Leif Eriksson, an early Viking explorer whose travels brought him to North America, wrote detailed descriptions of his encounters in the forests with ugly, hairy, dark-colored monsters with great black eyes. The *Exeter Watchman*, a New York newspaper, reported an account of the "Wild Man of the

Woods"[1] sighted near Ellisburgh on August 30, 1818. Even the highly regarded publication *Scientific American* told of a "Monstrous wild man"[2] in its March 1846 issue. The creature was said to have huge feet and was reportedly living in the swamps along the Missouri-Arkansas state line.

Bigfoot sightings were not unique to the eastern half of the United States. In the early 1920s the number of Bigfoot sightings increased on the western side of the country. In 1924 a group of miners working near Mount Saint Helens, Washington, experienced a Bigfoot encounter that created a new name for the area. The miners claimed they were approached by a Bigfoot when one of the men picked up a gun, then shot the creature. The miners went on to explain that on the same evening, they were surrounded and attacked by a swarm of angry Bigfoot creatures. The miners claimed that the beasts threw rocks at their cabin, pounded the walls, and stomped across the roof. The next day the fearful miners packed up their equipment and abandoned the cabin and mine. To this day, the area is known as Ape Canyon.

Although these accounts tell of sightings from long ago, reports of Bigfoot encounters continue today. Some experts claim an estimated ten Bigfoot encounters with humans occur around the world each week. Each year more than 550 Bigfoot sightings are reported in North America.

One of these encounters occurred in 1994 near Atwater, Ohio. A brother and sister decided to take

Sightings of huge, big-footed men in North America date back to the early explorers.

 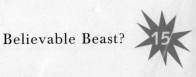

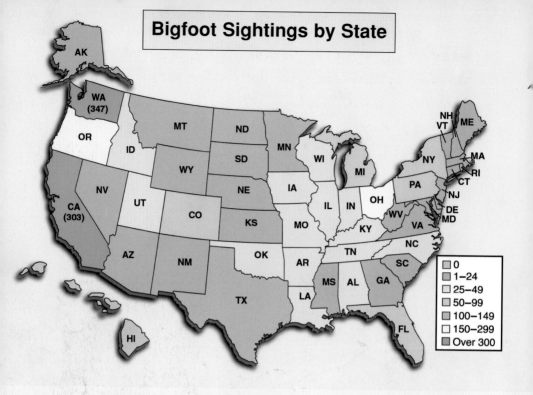

Bigfoot Sightings by State

WA (347)

CA (303)

Legend:
- 0
- 1–24
- 25–49
- 50–99
- 100–149
- 150–299
- Over 300

their motorcycle for a spin near an old strip-mining site when they spotted two Bigfeet walking near the road. "As soon as I realized that we were looking at two huge, two-legged things looking at us, I immediately got scared," the brother, known as "Rick J." stated. Rick J. explains that when the creatures realized they had been seen, they slipped into the woods and out of sight. He said, "In the distance we heard distinctly, branches breaking as if something snapped them as it ran."[3] Rick J. quickly restarted his motorcycle and he and his sister raced for home.

BIGFOOT'S BIG SUMMER

The summer of 2000 become known as the Summer of Sasquatch because it brought an extremely large

number of reported Bigfoot sightings. The media jumped on the stories and the reports seemed to flow nonstop from the spring through summer and fall until the attention began to quiet again in winter.

On March 28, 2000, one of the first accounts of that year was reported. A man delivering newspapers

This is a still shot from film taken in northern California in 1977 that reportedly shows Bigfoot walking in a clearing.

stated that he encountered a Bigfoot during the early morning hours near Granton, Wisconsin. James Hughes said that sometime around 5:00 A.M. he saw a creature near the road that appeared to be holding a goat under one arm. At first Hughes thought it was a large man, but as he moved closer, he realized the creature was about 8 feet (2.4m) tall with a face like

Many Bigfoot researchers dismiss this 1995 photo of a stocky Bigfoot standing in a forest as a hoax.

an ape. Hughes explains: "He was all covered with hair, a real dark gray color, with some spots that looked a honey color. It was walking on two legs, and it was mighty, mighty big." Struck with fear, Hughes sped away from the scene. "I didn't call it in [to the Sheriff's Department] until the next day because people would think I'm crazy. And I don't drink, I don't use dope, and I was wide awake."[4]

On July 1, 2000, psychologist Matthew Johnson shared his Bigfoot story with the press. While hiking with his family, Johnson stopped along the trail near the Oregon Caves National Monument in Selma, Oregon, to take a break. While standing near a tree, Johnson heard a grunting noise and smelled a strong, foul odor. Johnson explains: "I turned my head quickly and I saw this very tall, dark, hairy animal walk from behind one tree and over to another tree." Johnson instinctively ran to his family and hurried them away from the area. Later, Johnson described what he saw to reporters at the *Statesman Journal:* "I didn't immediately tell them what I saw. I didn't want to freak my kids out. I didn't want to freak my wife out." Johnson went on to say: "It was nothing else but a Sasquatch. I swear to God. I lived a lot of years in Alaska. I've been chased by a grizzly bear. This was no bear."[5]

After the Johnson story, reports of Bigfoot sightings began to pour in. One story tells of a late night in September, near Granite Falls, Washington, where Chris Wright stepped outside of his home. "I was not a firm believer in Bigfoot," said Wright. "But after last night, I'm rethinking that." As Wright stepped out into the yard, motion detectors turned on the security lights around his house. "At that point I heard a loud, high-pitched yell. I turned and looked to my right and that's when I saw him. I was looking right at the son of a gun," said Wright. Wright claims that the Bigfoot stood about 7 feet (2m) tall and was covered in dark hair. The creature ran into the woods. Wright was an experienced hunter and knew right away that the creature was not a bear. "Bears don't run like that,"[6] he said. Wright's momentary encounter with Bigfoot was one of the last sightings that year. The summer of Bigfoot was over.

Did You See That?

Since the summer of 2000, Bigfoot sightings have decreased but not stopped. The Bigfoot Field Research Organization, or BFRO, continuously collects eyewitness accounts of Bigfoot encounters. A former marine (who is also a retired firefighter and state police officer) said he saw a Bigfoot crossing a river in northern California on a sunny afternoon in August 2004. While driving along Highway 80 just west of Donner Pass, the witness, known only as F.H., spotted a tall figure in a ravine. F.H. reports: "I looked down and saw what looked like about a 7 to 8 foot (2 to 2.4m) tall, broad shouldered male." F.H. went on to explain that the figure was all black from head to toe. F.H. continues: "I immediately pulled over to the

Bigfoot

In this photo taken in Florida in 2000, a Bigfoot disappears into a swamp.

side of the roadway on the bridge and slowed so that I could see it better. It was walking in a lanky movement with arms swinging as it crossed the stream. Then I noticed a slightly smaller figure come out from the tree line."[7] F.H. watched the two creatures cross the stream until they disappeared into the trees on the other side.

This sampling of stories is small compared to the hundreds of reports gathered each year. Enthusiasts are convinced that the many tales of Bigfoot are true. Skeptics have tried to explain the stories away with logic and reason. One thing is certain. Those who claim to have seen Bigfoot are steadfast in their belief.

Believable Beast?

CHAPTER 3

TO PROVE OR DISPROVE

Thousands of scientists and enthusiasts work constantly to find facts and evidence to either prove or disprove the existence of a Bigfoot. Many people devote their entire lives to the quest for answers about the mysterious creature. Experts spend time analyzing film clips that supposedly show Bigfoot. They also measure and investigate footprints, construct and study plaster casts of footprints, and use special equipment to analyze samples supposedly made by Bigfoot.

THE PATTERSON/GIMLIN FILM

The piece of film shot by Roger Patterson and Robert Gimlin in October 1967 is considered by many experts to be the most believable evidence ever found to prove a Bigfoot's existence. Others swear the duo recorded nothing more than someone's elaborate joke.

Early studies of the film performed by film analyst Dmitri Donskoy of Moscow, Russia, and D.W. Grieve of London, England, concluded that the creature in the movie was most definitely not human. Both experts in human movement, Donskoy and Grieve stated that if the film was produced at a speed of 24 frames per second, it could possibly show a fast-walking human. But, the Patterson film was produced at a speed of 18 frames per second which captured a figure walking with a **gait** that Donskoy concluded was completely different from that of

Bigfoot has been spotted around the world. This is a drawing of the Australian Bigfoot, known locally as the yowie.

humans. Both Donskoy and Grieve agree that the creature in the film could in fact be Bigfoot.

Other respected experts agree that the film is authentic. Ken Peterson, who served as senior executive of Walt Disney Studios during the year the Patterson/Gimlin film was created, stated that even with Disney's state-of-the-art knowledge of special effects, his technicians would not be able to duplicate the creature shown in the film. More recently, enthusiasts from the BFRO have pointed out that the arms on the creature in the film are much too long to be that of a human dressed in an ape suit. Jeff Meldrum, associate professor of anatomy and anthropology at Idaho State University, claims, "It has been obvious to even the casual viewer that the film's subject possesses arms that are [too] long for its [height]."[8]

Pictured are three frames from the Patterson/Gimlin film, which was shot in 1967.

The film clip served to prove the existence of a Bigfoot until 2002, when a devastating blow was delivered to all Bigfoot enthusiasts. That was the year a man named Ray Wallace died. Near the end of his life Wallace, an amateur Bigfoot expert, claimed that he had produced the elaborate hoax to fool Patterson and Gimlin. The information became public after Wallace's death. Family members of Wallace explained that Wallace had suggested to Patterson where he should go to possibly catch a glimpse of Bigfoot. They went on to explain that the Bigfoot that Patterson filmed was actually one of Wallace's friends dressed in a realistic costume. To this day experts debate the authenticity of the Bigfoot shown in the film. Although many opinions have been formed, no one knows for certain what Patterson and Gimlin captured with their camera.

PERMANENT FOOTPRINTS

Capturing evidence on film is not the only way to study Bigfoot. Plaster can be a useful tool in gathering Bigfoot clues. Plaster is carefully poured into footprints left by a Bigfoot. The plaster is left to dry, then lifted out of the soil. An exact copy of each footprint is produced by the hard plaster and can be transported to labs where further study takes place. Hundreds of castings taken from sites all over the United States are collected in storehouses devoted to gathering Bigfoot evidence.

Jimmy Chilcutt, a forensic scientist from the Conroe, Texas, police department, took part in a

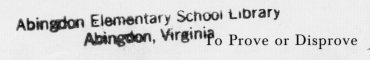

study designed to either prove or disprove the authenticity of the footprint casts. The sample footprints included in Chilcutt's study were taken from a collection of over 100 castings that were gathered from various locations and made over a span of more than twenty years. An expert on human fingerprint analysis, Chilcutt focused his energy on the dermal ridges found within the samples. With humans, the dermal ridges, or lines creating the footprint, tend to run side to side. Apes tend to have diagonal ridges running across their feet. The footprints used in Chilcutt's study had lengthwise ridges that were much wider and thicker than those found on human footprints. From the evidence he gathered, Chilcutt concluded that the dermal ridges found on the footprint samples in his study were not created by humans or any other known **primate**. It is his belief that there is an unknown great ape roaming the forests of North America. Chilcutt states, "I stake my reputation on it."[9]

Other methods of analyzing footprint data have also been used. Jeff Meldrum studied evidence from footprint analysis. His footprint samples came from groups of footprints found lined along a pathway. Trails of footprints suggest that the prints were created by the same creature walking in a straight line or path. By measuring specific points on these footprints, Meldrum was able to plot measurements on a graph. By charting the data, Meldrum concluded that the footprints did in fact come from some sort of

Footprints of a creature thought to be Bigfoot measure nearly sixteen inches in length in these casts.

animal and not a man-made costume. Meldrum states, "We may well have a large primate walking about in North American forests."[10]

Body Cast

Footprints are not the only images captured by enthusiasts toting buckets filled with plaster. In southern Washington in September 2000, a group of individuals set a trap in the mud near Skookum Meadows in Gifford Pinchot National Forest, where they hoped to

A $20 bill placed in a suspected Bigfoot footprint gives some idea how large the creature's feet might be.

capture a Bigfoot image. They claim to have been successful. By baiting the area with fruit, the group states, they were able to lure a Bigfoot into the mud, where it sat down and left a distinct impression in the soft soil. The group did not witness the creature first-hand, but they did manage to bring out a plaster cast of the half-body impression left behind. The impression is now known as the Skookum cast.

Meldrum led the study of the Skookum cast. During the investigation a heel imprint that measured much larger than any human footprint was found, along with hair samples and traces of saliva collected on chewed apple slices.

The samples of hair and saliva were sent to an independent lab for further investigation. No conclusive information could be determined by the lab's experiments. At some point in the process the samples were contaminated. Someone could have picked up the evidence with dirty hands, or a strand of human hair may have fallen in with the hair samples. No one is quite sure what happened, but the dirty samples yielded poor results.

SHRIEKS AND HOWLS

Not all evidence collected by Bigfoot enthusiasts can be seen. Some of the mysterious samples brought out of the woods can only be heard. Many enthusiasts believe that some of the shrieks, howls, and screams recorded by investigators are actually samples of Bigfoot sounds.

A sampling of such recordings was brought to bio-acoustics expert Robert Benson of Texas A&M, Corpus Christi. Using sophisticated instruments and computer printouts of sound waves, Benson was able to exclude a list of animals as sources of the sounds. Benson explains: "The sounds were definitely not produced by elk, owl, wolf, or coyote." He goes on to say that the sounds were "probably primate, but that of course includes humans as a possible source."[11]

Plagued by blurry images, contaminated samples, and inconclusive evidence, enthusiasts working to prove Bigfoot's existence have been met with frustration. Many people have devoted their lives to scouring the forests in search of the one piece of evidence that will, without question, put this mystery to rest. Will it be another footprint, a sample of hair, or a clear recording of a firsthand encounter with a live Bigfoot? One can only speculate if and how this incredible mystery will be solved.

CHAPTER 4

MYSTERY AND MERCHANDISE

The mysterious stories of Bigfoot have grabbed the attention of people all over the world. Bigfoot legends are so popular that merely mentioning the beast's name sparks clear images of a huge and hairy, big-footed creature in almost everyone's mind.

Thanks to the efforts of some creative people, the image of Bigfoot does not have to be left up to the imagination. From hats and backpacks decorated with Bigfoot images to welcome mats that sport giant footprints, there is no shortage of Bigfoot merchandise. One company proudly displays its own Bigfoot Action Figure. A toy geared for both children and adults, the Bigfoot Action Figure is equipped with footprint stamps on the bottom of its feet for "real footprint action."[12] Bigfoot fans can advertise their enthusiasm by wearing Bigfoot T-shirts or carrying their keys on a miniplaster footprint keychain. Those who are serious about gathering their own Bigfoot evidence can purchase a research kit complete with disposable camera, plaster, and specimen bags.

BIGFOOT ON THE BIG SCREEN

After spending a day in the woods collecting evidence, Bigfoot fans can choose to sit back and enjoy a movie starring Bigfoot himself. Amateur filmmakers Charles B. Pierce and Earl E. Smith wrote and produced the film *The Legend of Boggy Creek* after an encounter with what they believed to be a Bigfoot in a swamp near Fouke, Arkansas. The movie questions the existence of Bigfoot in Arkansas. Although produced by amateurs, the 1973 film has developed a sizable fan base. Many Bigfoot enthusiasts consider it an unrealistic yet fun film.

Hollywood filmmakers have also been inspired by Bigfoot. The 1987 film *Harry and the Hendersons* tells the story of a family who, while driving home from a vacation, slams into an unsuspecting Bigfoot with the car. Both saddened and thrilled with their discovery, they strap the Bigfoot to the hood of the car and bring it home. Upon their return, the Bigfoot

This wax figure of a Bigfoot is part of a traveling show in eastern Europe.

In the 1987 film Harry and the Hendersons, *Bigfoot is a highly sensitive and lovable creature.*

wakes up. The family feels guilty for causing the animal harm and decides to let their new furry friend, whom they name Harry, move in with them. Harry turns out to be a sensitive and charming fellow and, in the end, is returned to the forest.

BIG GATHERINGS

Bigfoot enthusiasts determined to prove that Bigfoot is more than just a fictional character gather each year at conferences and meetings across the United States. Several Bigfoot conferences are held in places like Newcomerstown, Ohio; Carson, Washington;

and Conroe, Texas. Hundreds of people pack convention centers to listen to guest speakers, visit merchandise booths, and share their own stories with other Bigfoot fans. Terry Altman, president of the Pennsylvania Bigfoot Society, comments on a recent conference, "I'd say half the people here are researchers and members of our group. The others are curiosity-seekers or just interested."[13] John A. Bindernagel, a conference speaker and Bigfoot believer, describes his conference experiences as "Almost like a support group, letting people know its okay to see a Bigfoot. You don't have to be embarrassed."[14]

Workers set up the main stage at a 1997 Sasquatch convention held in Vancouver, Canada.

Not all conference attendees go to these events to share stories. Some people go to learn. Bigfoot enthusiasts attend classes where they are taught how to properly gather evidence, make plaster track impressions, and test hair samples. Conference attendees can also learn about new, state-of-the-art **surveillance equipment**. William Dranginis of Manassas, Virginia, recently developed and displayed a new four-camera remote-controlled surveillance system. He hopes to capture film footage of Bigfoot by bringing his system to an area where he once spotted an unknown creature. When the cameras are set up, a signal will tell Dranginis when Bigfoot is near. Dranginis can then maneuver the cameras with his laptop computer and, he hopes, capture a clear image of Bigfoot on film.

Not all Bigfoot events are educational or scientific. Some are held simply for fun. One year the picnic menu for the Bigfoot Daze celebration in Carson, Washington, included items such as Bigfoot burgers, abominable potato salad, and yeti spaghetti. After the picnic, Bigfoot fans were invited to take part in the Bigfoot Stomp dance contest. Some celebrations include Bigfoot screaming contests. Bigfoot costume contests have inspired people to create furry outfits for the whole family. One celebration ended with a Bigfoot race. Teams of participants strapped on giant feet and raced to the finish in a competition for Bigfoot-themed prizes.

For people who would rather stay away from the crowds that conventions can attract, a resort or lodge

named after Bigfoot may provide the perfect place for relaxation. Campgrounds and lodges with names such as the Sasquatch Inn, Bigfoot Retreat Bed and Breakfast, and Bigfoot Campground, are scattered throughout the U.S. Pacific Northwest and Canada's British Columbia. Green Point Park, near Harrison Hot Springs, British Columbia, was renamed Sasquatch Park. Several reports of Bigfoot sightings in the area prompted the official name change.

A Bigfoot enthusiast poses next to the Sasquatch Drive road sign in British Columbia, Canada.

BIGFOOT ON THE WEB

Bigfoot fans who would rather not travel can find exciting Bigfoot information on the Internet. There are several interesting Web sites that Bigfoot enthusiasts can use to keep up-to-date with current findings as well as share their own stories. The most notable Bigfoot Web site is hosted by the BFRO. Visitors to this

In this illustration, a yeti walks through the snow of the Himalayas. In the minds of believers around the world, Bigfoot truly exists.

site can read firsthand accounts of Bigfoot sightings, investigate stacks of research, sign up to attend a Bigfoot search expedition, or even report their own experiences with a Bigfoot. The BFRO Web site also includes samples of supposed Bigfoot videos, maps that plot hundreds of Bigfoot sightings throughout the United States, and scores of recent Bigfoot articles found in the media. For those who want to know more about Bigfoot, the BFRO Web site is the place to go.

Even with thousands of people studying footprint evidence, examining photographs, and investigating eyewitness encounters, the Bigfoot mystery has yet to be proved or disproved. There is no doubt that researchers and enthusiasts will continue to scour forests, hoping to catch a glimpse of the elusive creature and bring back a Bigfoot story of their own. Many people will remain skeptical of the stories unless a Bigfoot is captured and brought to the attention of the entire world. Others do not require such drastic measures in order to be convinced that Bigfoot is a true, living being. For those who claim to have seen one, there is no question—Bigfoot lives!

NOTES

CHAPTER 2: BELIEVABLE BEAST?

1. Quoted in Loren Coleman, *BIGFOOT! The True Story of Apes in America.* New York: Paraview, 2003, p. 36.
2. Quoted in Coleman, *BIGFOOT!*, p. 36.
3. Quoted in *BFRO Online*, "Bigfoot Reports." www.bfro.net/GDB/show_report.asp?id=359.
4. Quoted in Coleman, *BIGFOOT!*, p. 12.
5. Quoted in Coleman, *BIGFOOT!*, p. 14.
6. Quoted in Coleman, *BIGFOOT!*, p. 15.
7. Quoted in *BFRO Online*, "Report #9555." www.bfro.net/GDB/show_report.asp?id=9555.

CHAPTER 3: TO PROVE OR DISPROVE

8. Jeff Meldrum, *BFRO Online*. www.bfro.net/news/challenge/green.asp.
9. Quoted in *Sasquatch: Legend Meets Science,* DVD, Whitewolf Entertainment, 2003.
10. Quoted in *Sasquatch*.
11. Quoted in *Sasquatch*.

CHAPTER 4: MYSTERY AND MERCHANDISE

12. Bigfoot Surplus, "Bigfoot Action Figure." www.

bigfootsurplus.com/bigfoot_tracker/03-0009. php.

13. Quoted in Rebekah Scott, "Bigfoot Believers Gather in Jeannette," *Bigfoot: Fact or Fantasy?* www.rfthomas.clara.net/news/jeanette.html.

14. Quoted in *Plain Dealer,* Newcomerstown, Ohio, "Bigfoot Convention Report," Cactus Ventures. www.cactusventures.com/webstuff5/bigfoot_ convention_report.htm.

GLOSSARY

bipedal: Having two feet and normally walking in an upright position.

cast: A replica made by pouring plaster into a footprint.

gait: The manner in which a person or creature walks.

hominids: All humanlike creatures, including man and his ancestors.

primate: Any member of the group of mammals that includes humans, apes, and monkeys.

Sasquatch: Canadian word used to describe a Bigfoot-type creature.

surveillance equipment: Equipment used to watch over a designated area.

yeti: Name used in China, Tibet, and Scotland for a Bigfoot-type creature.

FOR FURTHER EXPLORATION

BOOKS

Greg Long, *The Making of Bigfoot: The Inside Story*. Amherst, NY: Prometheus, 2003. In this book Long presents his explanation for the Patterson/Gimlin Bigfoot footage and tries to convince others that it was all a hoax.

L.L. Owens, *Bigfoot: The Legend Lives On*. Logan, IA: Perfection Learning, 1999. Packed full of anecdotes and legends, this book will help explain why so many people believe in Bigfoot.

Philip L. Rife, *Bigfoot Across America*. Lincoln, NE: iUniverse, 2000. Read some of the most amazing Bigfoot stories describing encounters across the United States.

WEB SITES

The Bigfoot Field Researchers Organization (www.bfro.net). Look at this Web site to find out how many Bigfoot sightings have been reported in your own state. This site also includes firsthand stories of hundreds of Bigfoot encounters.

The Museum of Unnatural Mystery (www. unmuseum.com). Click on the index button, then scroll down to "Bigfoot" to find a page that tells about Native American Bigfoot legends. This Web site also include a diagram of a Bigfoot footprint compared to an adult human male.

The Skeptic's Dictionary (www.skepdic.com). This Web site gives information to disprove the Bigfoot theories. Search for Bigfoot to find information about how some Bigfoot evidence could be fake.

VIDEO

Sasquatch: The Legend Meets Science, DVD, Whitewolf Entertainment, 2003. This DVD, first shown on the Discovery Channel, explains the investigations into several Bigfoot stories using modern technology.

INDEX

Altman, Terry, 35
Ape Canyon (Washington), 14
appearance, 9–10, 19, 20–21, 24
arms, 10, 21, 24

Benson, Robert, 30
Beowulf, 7–8
Bigfoot Action Figure, 31–32
Bigfoot Daze celebration, 36
Bigfoot Field Research
  Organization (BFRO), 20,
  38–39
Bindernagel, John A., 35
bipedal walking, 9, 19, 21,
  23–24

campgrounds, 36–37
Canada, 6–7
celebrations, 36
Chilcutt, Jimmy, 25–26
communication, 10
conferences, 34–36
Crew, Jeffrey, 6

diet, 10–11
Donskoy, Dmitri, 23–24
Dranginis, William, 36

Eriksson, Leif, 13
evidence
  films, 4–6, 22–25
  footprints, 6, 25–26, 28–29
  sound recordings, 29–30
  surveillance equipment for, 36
Exeter Watchman (newspaper),
  13–14
explanations, 9

F.H., 20–21
films, 4–6, 22–25
footprints, 6, 25–26, 28–29

Gifford Pinchot National Forest
  (Washington), 28–29
Gimlin, Robert, 5–6, 22–25
Grendel, 7–8
Grieve, D.W., 23–24

hair, 9–10, 19, 20
Harry and the Hendersons (film),
  32, 34
hominid theory, 9
Hughes, James, 18–19
Humboldt Times (newspaper), 6
Hupa (Native Americans), 9

Internet, 38–39

Johnson, Matthew, 19

Legend of Boggy Creek, The (film), 32
legends, 7–9, 31
lodges, 36–37

Meldrum, Jeff, 24, 26, 28, 29
merchandise, 31–32
Mount Saint Helens, Washington, 14
movies, 32, 34

name, 6

Omah (demon of the wilderness), 9

Patterson, Roger, 4–6, 22–25
Peterson, Ken, 24
Pierce, Charles B., 32
plaster casts, 6, 25–26, 28–29
popularity, 31

Qah-lin-me (the devourer), 9
research kits, 32

Rick J., 16

Sasquatch, 6–7
Scientific American (magazine), 14
sightings, 4–7, 13–14, 16–21, 32
Six Rivers National Forest (California), 4–5
size, 6, 10, 18, 20
skin, 9
Skookum cast, 29
smell, 10, 19
Smith, Earl E., 32
sound recordings, 29–30
Statesman Journal (newspaper), 19
Summer of Sasquatch, 16–20
surveillance equipment, 36

toys, 31–32

Wallace, Ray, 25
Web sites, 38–39
"Wild Man of the Woods" (newspaper account), 13–14
Wright, Chris, 19–20

Yakama (Native Americans), 9
yeti, 7

PICTURE CREDITS

ABOUT THE AUTHOR

Heather L. Miller has written several books for KidHaven Press. *Bigfoot* is her first in the Monsters series. Miller lives in northeast Indiana with her husband, two daughters, and two dogs, where she enjoys teaching art and writing stories for children. She has yet to experience her first Bigfoot encounter.